# Baby's First Bible Story Book

Speedy Publishing LLC
40 E. Main St. #1156
Newark, DE 19711

www.speedypublishing.com

Copyright 2014
9781681275543
First Printed January 9, 2015

# The Birth of Jesus

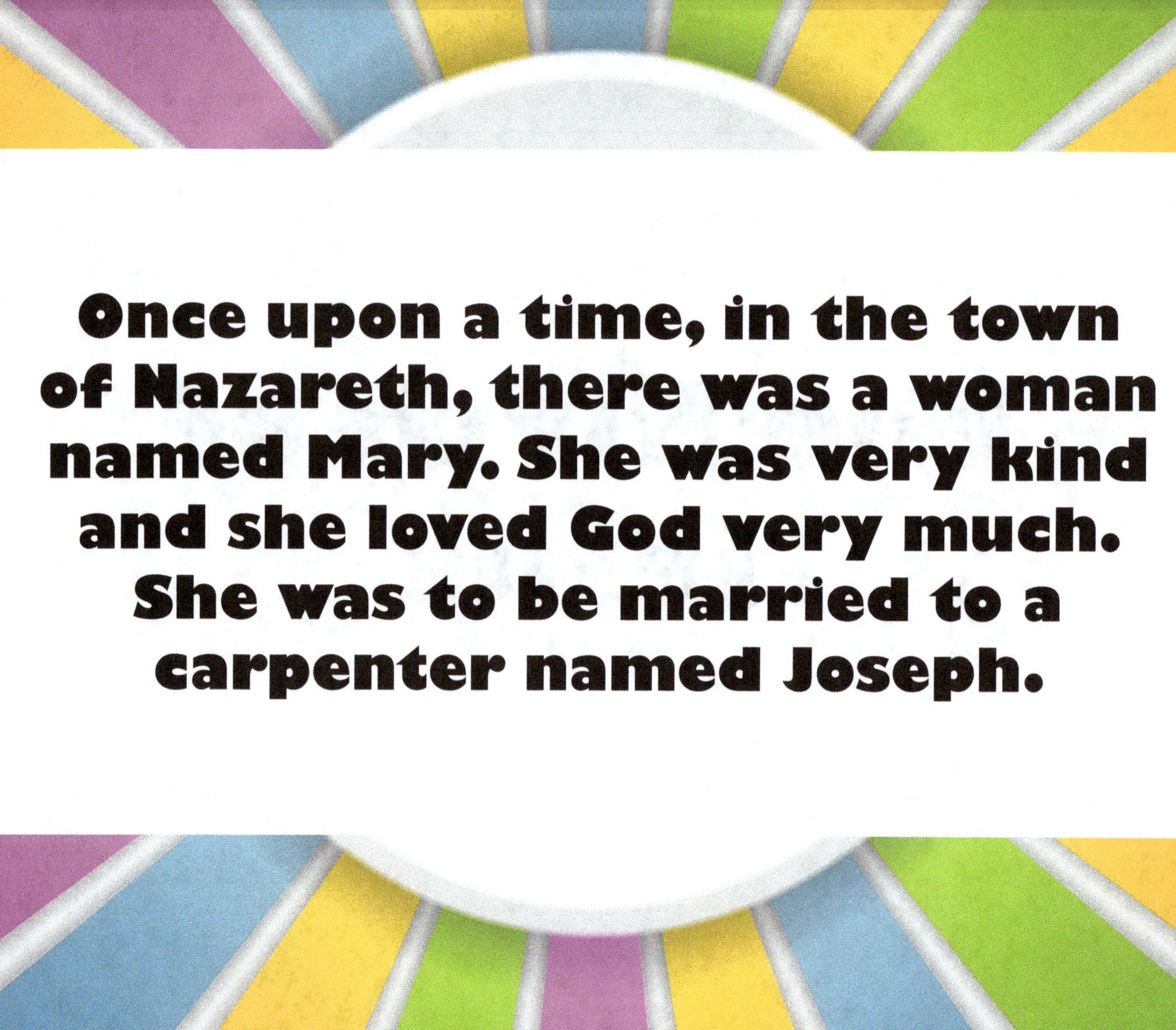

Once upon a time, in the town of Nazareth, there was a woman named Mary. She was very kind and she loved God very much. She was to be married to a carpenter named Joseph.

One day, an angel appeared to Mary and told her she will have a baby boy and it will be named Jesus. It was truly a miracle because she conceived through the Holy Spirit and because the baby will be called the Son of God. Mary trembled and knelt down and said she will serve the Lord with all her heart. The angel also visited Joseph and the angel told him to take Mary as his wife and to take care of the son of God that will be named Jesus.

That time, Mary and Joseph decided to flee Nazareth because it was not safe for Mary to give birth there. They went to Bethlehem and looked for a place to stay because Mary will soon give birth to Jesus. They did not find any place to stay but someone took them in a small barn where animas were kept.

It was the night where Jesus was born in the manger. There was a bright shining star glowing in the sky at the time Jesus was born. And today we celebrate Jesus' birthday as Christmas!

# Jesus, the son of God

# The Beatitudes

## Matthew 5:1-12

Now when he saw the crowds, he went up on a mountainside and sat down. His disciples came to Him, and He began to teach them, saying:

**Blessed are the poor in spirit, for theirs is the kingdom of heaven.**

Blessed are those who mourn, for they will be comforted.

Blessed are the meek, for they will inherit the earth.

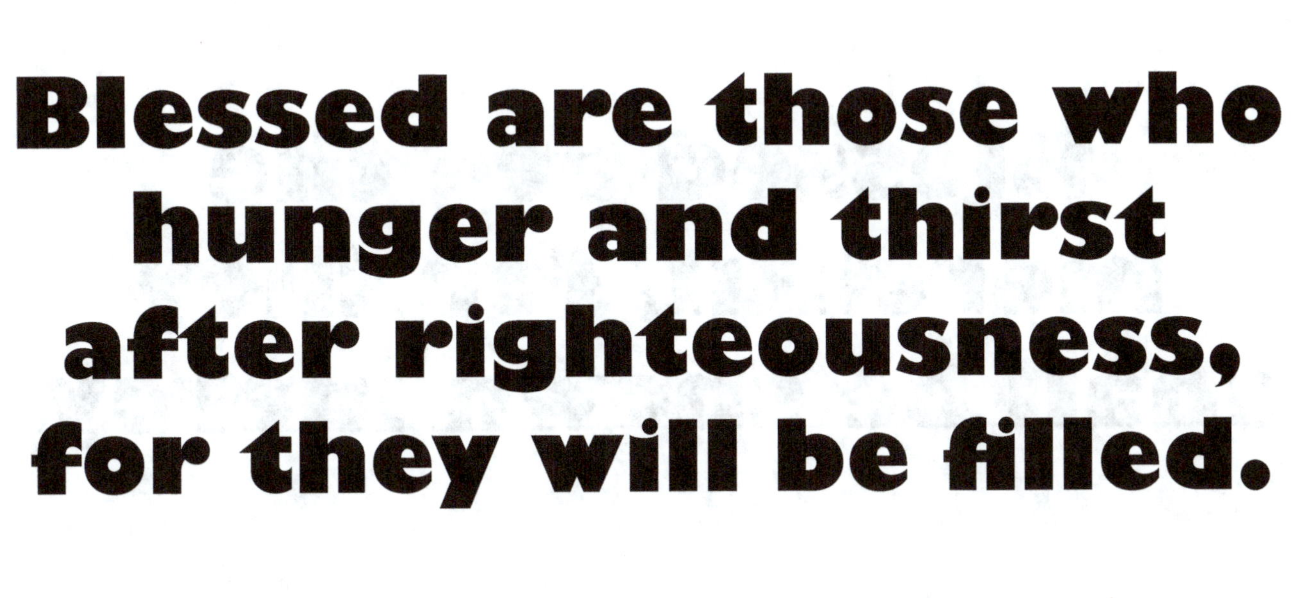

Blessed are those who hunger and thirst after righteousness, for they will be filled.

**Blessed are the merciful, for they shall be shown mercy.**

**Blessed are the pure in heart, for they will see God.**

**Blessed are the peacemakers, for they will be called the sons of God.**

Blessed are those who are persecuted because of righteousness, for theirs is the kingdom of heaven.

Blessed are you when people insult you, persecute you and falsely say all kinds of evil against you because of me.

Rejoice and be glad, because great is your reward in heaven, for in the same way they persecuted the prophets who were before you.

"Let the wise listen and add to their learning."
Proverbs 1:5

# How to be wise?

# Proverbs 1:1-7

**Being smart is knowing things.  Being wise is doing the smart things you know. Proverbs tells us:**

**to listen to the things our parents teach us (1:8)**
**to listen to when people correct us or tell us a better way to do things (1:3)**
**a fool doesn't want to listen to wise teaching or correction (1:7)**
**wise people will get even smarter (1:5)**

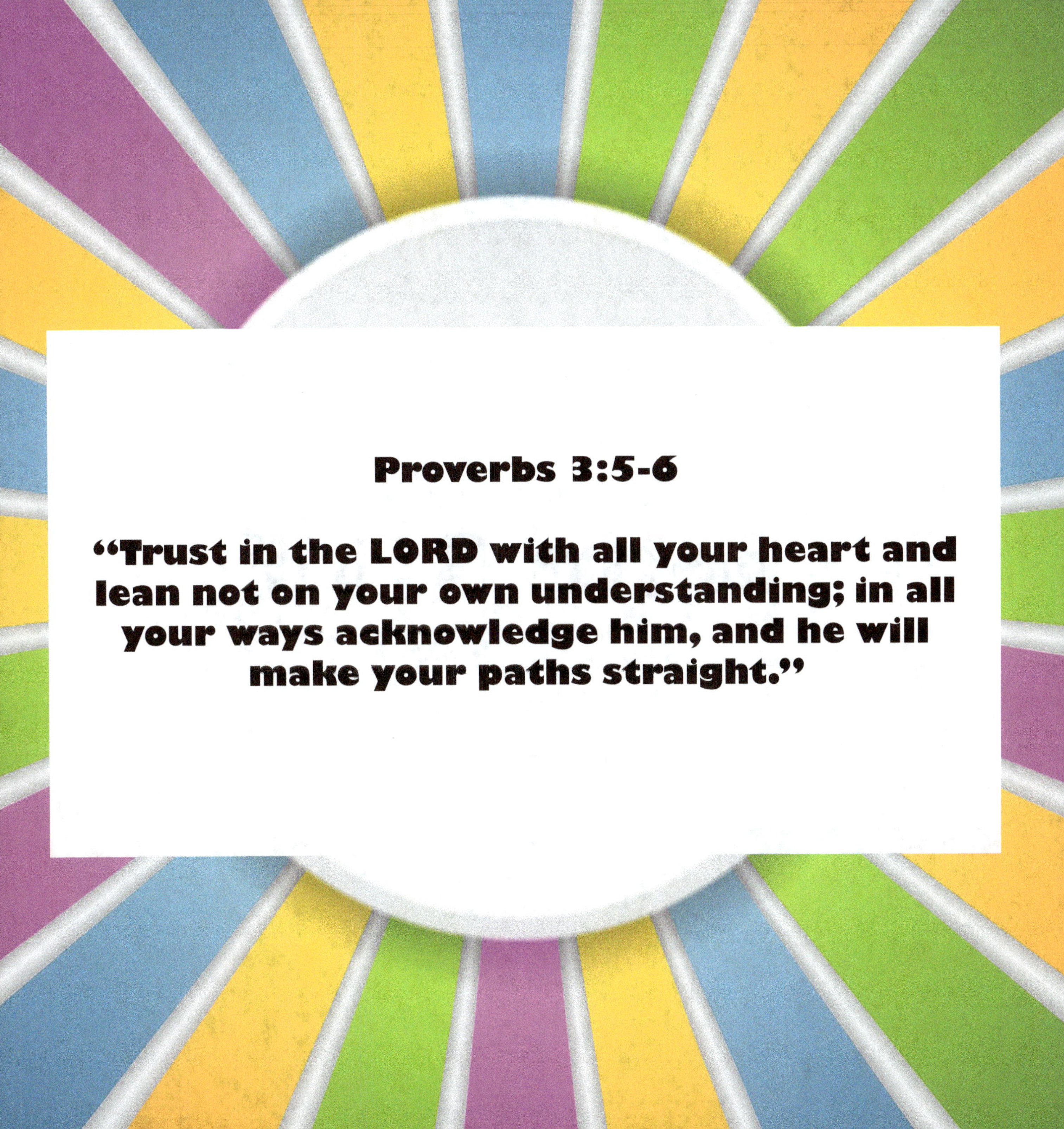

Proverbs 3:5-6
"Trust in the LORD with all your heart and lean not on your own understanding; in all your ways acknowledge him, and he will make your paths straight."

# John 3:16

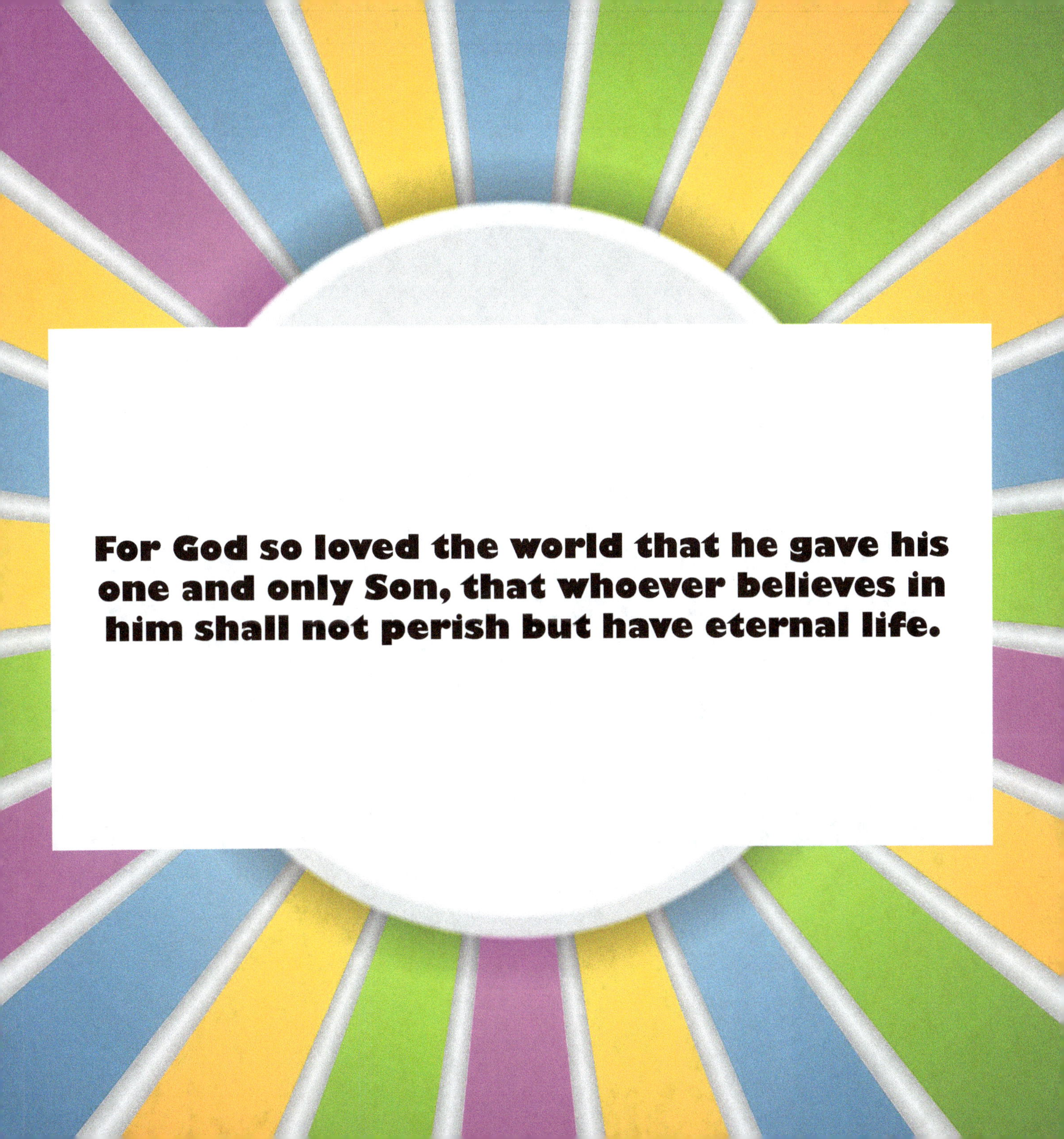

For God so loved the world that he gave his one and only Son, that whoever believes in him shall not perish but have eternal life.